The Ro
Our Lady

CW01467525

A manual of devotion

Compiled for the
Rosary Confraternity of Our Lady of Glastonbury

Edited by Johnathon Moses

Contents

How to say the Rosary
4

Why is the Rosary so effectual?
5

Rosary Prayers
8

Rosary Prayers in Latin
10

The Mysteries of the Rosary
12

Scriptural Rosary: Joyful Mysteries
13

Scriptural Rosary: Sorrowful Mysteries
23

Scriptural Rosary: Glorious Mysteries
33

Litany of the Blessed Virgin Mary
44

Rosary Office for the Dead
47

The Angelus
49

The Magnificat
51

The Magnificat in Latin
52

How to Say the Rosary

The Rosary really consists of fifteen decades, and each decade is made up of one Our Father, ten Hail Marys, and one "Glory be to the Father." Thus the complete Rosary consists of fifteen "Pater Nosters" *and* "Glorias," and one hundred and fifty "Ave Marias." This devotion is usually, though not necessarily, recited on beads, and it is highly recommended to have these beads blessed and indulgenced. It has been stated above that, while reciting each decade, we meditate on some particular mystery in the lives of Jesus and Mary.

Custom has divided the Rosary into three parts, each of which consists of five decades.

In fact, when we now speak of saying the Rosary, we generally refer to the recitation of five decades, and the Rosary beads are arranged accordingly.

The three parts of the Rosary commemorate respectively the joyful, the sorrowful and the glorious mysteries in the lives of Jesus and Mary; hence there are five joyful, five sorrowful, and five glorious mysteries.

The Joyful Mysteries are assigned to Mondays and Thursdays throughout the year and to the Sundays of Advent, as well as to the Sundays from the Feast of the Epiphany until Lent. The Sorrowful Mysteries are prescribed for Tuesdays and Fridays, and for the Sundays in Lent.

The Glorious Mysteries are designated for Wednesdays and Saturdays, and for the Sundays from Easter to Advent.

Hail Mary

Hail Mary, full of grace, the Lord is with thee. Blessed art thou among women, and blessed is the fruit of thy womb, Jesus. Holy Mary, Mother of God, pray for us sinners, now and at the hour of our death. Amen.

Glory Be

GLORY BE to the Father, and to the Son, and to the Holy Spirit. As it was in the beginning is now, and ever shall be, world without end. Amen.

Hail Holy Queen

Hail Holy Queen, mother of mercy; our life, our sweetness, and our hope. To thee do we cry, poor banished children of Eve. To thee do we send up our sighs, mourning and weeping in this vale of tears. Turn, then, most gracious advocate, thine eyes of mercy toward us. And after this, our exile, show unto us the blessed fruit of thy womb, Jesus. O clement, O loving, O sweet Virgin Mary. Pray for us, O holy Mother of God, that we may be made worthy of the promises of Christ. Amen.

Rosary Prayers in Latin

Invocation

In nomine Patris et Filii et Spiritus Sancti. Amen.

Symbolum Apostolorum - Apostles Creed

Crédo in Déum, Pátrem omnipoténtem, Creatórem cáeli et térræ. Et in Jésum Chrístum, Fílium éjus unícum, Dóminum nóstrum, qui concéptus est de Spíritu Sáncto, nátus ex María Vírgine, pássus sub Póntio Piláto, crucifíxus, mórtuus, et sepúltus. Descéndit ad ínferos: tértia díe resurréxit a mórtuis: ascéndit ad cáelos: sédet ad déxteram Déi Pátris omnipoténtis: índe ventúrus est judicáre vívos et mórtuos.

Crédo in Spíritum Sánctum, sánctam Ecclésiam Cathólicam, Sanctórum communiónem, remissiónem peccatórum, cárnis resurrectiónem, vítam ætérnam. Amen.

Pater noster - Our Father

Páter nóster, qui es in cáelis, sanctificétur nómen túum. Advéniat régnum túum. Fíat volúntas túa, sícut in cáelo et in térra. Pánem nóstrum quotidiánum da nóbis hódie, et dimítte nóbis débita nóstra, sícut et nos dimíttimus debitóribus nóstris. Et ne nos indúcas in tentatiónem: sed líbera nos a málo. Amen.

It is customary to commence the Rosary by reciting the Apostles' Creed, one "Our Father," three "Hail Marys," and one "Glory be to the Father." We then proceed to the five decades with the respective mysteries.

At the beginning of each decade a brief outline of the mystery is often read in order to help us to fix our mind upon that particular mystery while reciting the decade. At the end of each decade, before announcing and reading the reflection on the following mystery, a suitable prayer regarding the fruit to be derived from the previous decade is frequently recited.

At the end of the five decades the "Hail, Holy Queen" is generally said.

Why the Rosary Is So Effectual

The great means of salvation and sanctification, the means which God has established for procuring efficacious grace to resist every temptation and acquire every virtue, the means that fertilizes, so to say, the sacerdotal ministry, is prayer. We need but read the Gospels attentively to be persuaded of this truth. Now, there are two kinds of prayer, mental and vocal, which consist respectively in pious reflection or meditation on the mysteries of our faith, and in earnest petition for graces both for ourselves and for others. The Rosary beautifully unites these two kinds, and is thus a perfect form of prayer. And it derives special efficacy from the fact that it is directed to the Mother of God, whose intercession on our behalf before the Throne of Grace is endowed with extraordinary power, so that Mary is fittingly called

"Mother of Divine Grace," and "All-powerful Suppliant."

In the Rosary we survey, or rather ponder on, the entire series of mysteries enacted in the lives of Jesus and Mary from the moment of the Incarnation until the Coronation of the Queen of Heaven. In the Joyful Mysteries we contemplate Mary becoming the Mother of the Word made flesh, visiting her cousin St. Elizabeth, bringing forth the Saviour of men, offering to God the Infant Jesus as a tender victim, and finding Him, after the three days' loss, in the temple of Jerusalem. The Sorrowful Mysteries set before our minds the Incarnate Word agonizing in the Garden of Olives for love of us, undergoing an inhuman scourging in Pilate's hall, wearing a thorny crown of ignominy, laden with a heavy cross, and finally sacrificing His life, in supreme anguish, on Calvary for our redemption. In the Glorious Mysteries we consider Christ's triumphant resurrection and ascension, the coming of the Holy Ghost, the Comforter, and the assumption and coronation of the Virgin Mother.

Who shall measure, or even describe the salutary influence which the successive prayerful contemplation of these fifteen mysteries exercises on the soul? Do we not thereby literally steep our mind and will and heart in the most sacred truths of Christianity, and thus flood our souls with celestial light, strengthened them with supernatural unction?

While our mind is engaged in the contemplation of the mysteries of the Rosary, we devoutly recite the Hail Mary; which is at once a salutation and an invocation—a salutation that was first addressed to the Holy Virgin by an Archangel inspired by the

Blessed Trinity, and an invocation imploring Mary's constant protection during life, and her powerful assistance in our dying moments. The Hail Mary is as it were the heavenly anthem whose sweet strains accompany the contemplation of the touching mysteries of the lives of Jesus and Mary. It is the prayer that gives most honor to the Immaculate Maiden, and which most effectually procures for us her powerful help, and hence it is a prayer that Mary's children delight in offering their heavenly Mother.

Excerpted from "The Rosary: Its History and How to Say It", by Michael Davitt Forrest (1926)

Rosary Prayers

Invocation
In the name of the Father, and of the Son, and of the Holy Spirit. Amen.

The Apostles Creed
I believe in God, the Father almighty, Creator of Heaven and earth.

And in Jesus Christ, His only Son, our Lord, Who was conceived by the Holy Spirit, born of the Virgin Mary, suffered under Pontius Pilate; was crucified, died, and was buried. He descended into Hell. The third day He rose again from the dead. He ascended into Heaven, and sits at the right hand of God, the Father almighty. He shall come again to judge the living and the dead.

I believe in the Holy Spirit, the holy Catholic Church, the communion of saints, the forgiveness of sins, the resurrection of the body, and life everlasting. Amen.

Our Father
Our Father, Who art in Heaven, hallowed be Thy Name. Thy kingdom come, Thy will be done on earth as it is in Heaven. Give us this day our daily bread, and forgive us our trespasses, as we forgive those who trespass against us. And lead us not into temptation, but deliver us from evil. Amen.

Hail Mary

Hail Mary, full of grace, the Lord is with thee. Blessed art thou among women, and blessed is the fruit of thy womb, Jesus. Holy Mary, Mother of God, pray for us sinners, now and at the hour of our death. Amen.

Glory Be

GLORY BE to the Father, and to the Son, and to the Holy Spirit. As it was in the beginning is now, and ever shall be, world without end. Amen.

Hail Holy Queen

Hail Holy Queen, mother of mercy; our life, our sweetness, and our hope. To thee do we cry, poor banished children of Eve. To thee do we send up our sighs, mourning and weeping in this vale of tears. Turn, then, most gracious advocate, thine eyes of mercy toward us. And after this, our exile, show unto us the blessed fruit of thy womb, Jesus. O clement, O loving, O sweet Virgin Mary. Pray for us, O holy Mother of God, that we may be made worthy of the promises of Christ. Amen.

Rosary Prayers in Latin

Invocation
In nomine Patris et Filii et Spiritus Sancti. Amen.

Symbolum Apostolorum - Apostles Creed

Crédo in Déum, Pátrem omnipoténtem, Creatórem cáeli et térræ. Et in Jésum Chrístum, Fílium éjus unícum, Dóminum nóstrum, qui concéptus est de Spíritu Sáncto, nátus ex María Vírgine, pássus sub Póntio Piláto, crucifíxus, mórtuus, et sepúltus. Descéndit ad ínferos: tértia díe resurréxit a mórtuis: ascéndit ad cáelos: sédet ad déxteram Déi Pátris omnipoténtis: índe ventúrus est judicáre vívos et mórtuos.

Crédo in Spíritum Sánctum, sánctam Ecclésiam Cathólicam, Sanctórum communiónem, remissiónem peccatórum, cárnis resurrectiónem, vítam ætérnam. Amen.

Pater noster - Our Father
Páter nóster, qui es in cáelis, sanctificétur nómen túum. Advéniat régnum túum. Fíat volúntas túa, sícut in cáelo et in térra. Pánem nóstrum quotidiánum da nóbis hódie, et dimítte nóbis débita nóstra, sícut et nos dimíttimus debitóribus nóstris. Et ne nos indúcas in tentatiónem: sed líbera nos a málo. Amen.

Ave Maria - Hail Mary

Áve María, grátia pléna, Dóminus técum; benedícta tu in muliéribus, et benedíctus frúctus véntris túi, Jésus. Sáncta María, Máter Déi, óra pro nóbis peccatóribus, nunc et in hóra mórtis nóstræ. Amen.

Gloria Patri- Glory be

Glória Pátri, et Fílio, et Spirítui Sáncto. Sícut érat in princípio et nunc et sémper et in sáecula sæculórum. Amen.

Salve Regina - Hail, Holy Queen

Sálve Regína, máter misericórdiæ: víta, dulcédo, et spes nóstra, sálve. Ad te clamámus, exsúles fílii Hévæ. Ad te suspirámus, geméntes et fléntes in hac lacrimárum válle. Éja érgo, Advocáta nóstra, íllos túos misericórdes óculos ad nos convérte. Et Jésum, benedíctum frúctum véntris túi, nóbis post hoc exsílium osténde. O clémens, O pía, O dúlcis Vírgo María, Óra pro nóbis sáncta Déi Génitrix ut dígni efficiámur promissiónibus Chrísti.

The Mysteries of the Rosary

The Five Joyful Mysteries
Said on Mondays; Thursdays; Sundays of Advent, Christmastide and Time After Epiphany
The Annunciation
The Visitation
The Nativity
The Presentation
The Finding of Jesus in the Temple

The Five Sorrowful Mysteries
Said on Tuesdays; Fridays; all the days of Septuagesima and Lent
The Agony in the Garden
The Scourging
The Crowning with thorns
The Carrying of the Cross
The Crucifixion

The Five Glorious Mysteries
Said on Wednesdays; Saturdays; Sundays of Eastertide and Time After Pentecost
The Resurrection
The Ascension
The Pentecost
The Assumption
The Coronation of Mary

A Scriptural Rosary

The Five Joyful Mysteries

The First Joyful Mystery - The Annunciation

Our Father/Pater noster

And in the sixth month, the angel Gabriel was sent from God into a city of Galilee, called Nazareth, To a virgin espoused to a man whose name was Joseph, of the house of David; and the virgin's name was Mary.

Hail Mary/Ave

And the angel being come in, said unto her: Hail, full of grace, the Lord is with thee: blessed art thou among women.

Hail Mary/Ave

Who having heard, was troubled at his saying, and thought with herself what manner of salutation this should be.

Hail Mary/Ave

And the angel said to her: Fear not, Mary, for thou hast found grace with God.

Hail Mary/Ave

Behold thou shalt conceive in thy womb, and shalt bring forth a son; and thou shalt call his name Jesus.

Hail Mary/Ave

He shall be great, and shall be called the Son of the most High; and the Lord God shall give unto him the throne of David his father; and he shall reign in the house of Jacob for ever. And of his kingdom there shall be no end.

Hail Mary/Ave

And Mary said to the angel: How shall this be done, because I know not man?

Hail Mary/Ave

And the angel answering, said to her: The Holy Ghost shall come upon thee, and the power of the most High shall overshadow thee.

Hail Mary/Ave

And therefore also the Holy which shall be born of thee shall be called the Son of God.

Hail Mary/Ave

And Mary said: Behold the handmaid of the Lord; be it done to me according to thy word. And the angel departed from her.

Hail Mary/Ave

Glory be/Gloria Patri

The Second Joyful Mystery - The Visitation

Our Father/Pater noster

And Mary rising up in those days, went into the hill country with haste into a city of Juda. And she entered into the house of Zachary, and saluted Elizabeth.

Hail Mary/Ave

And it came to pass, that when Elizabeth heard the salutation of Mary, the infant leaped in her womb. And Elizabeth was filled with the Holy Ghost.

Hail Mary/Ave

And she cried out with a loud voice, and said: Blessed art thou among women, and blessed is the fruit of thy womb.

Hail Mary/Ave

And blessed art thou that hast believed, because those things shall be accomplished that were spoken to thee by the Lord.

Hail Mary/Ave

And Mary said: My soul doth magnify the Lord. And my spirit hath rejoiced in God my Saviour. Because he hath regarded the humility of his handmaid; for behold from henceforth all generations shall call me blessed.

Hail Mary/Ave

Because he that is mighty, hath done great things to me; and holy is his name.

Hail Mary/Ave

And his mercy is from generation unto generations, to them that fear him.

Hail Mary/Ave

He hath shewed might in his arm: he hath scattered the proud in the conceit of their heart.

Hail Mary/Ave

He hath put down the mighty from their seat, and hath exalted the humble.

Hail Mary/Ave

He hath filled the hungry with good things; and the rich he hath sent empty away.

Hail Mary/Ave

Glory be/Gloria Patri

The Third Joyful Mystery - The Nativity

Our Father/Pater noster

And it came to pass, that when they were there, her days were accomplished, that she should be delivered.

Hail Mary/Ave

And she brought forth her firstborn son, and wrapped him up in swaddling clothes, and laid him in a manger; because there was no room for them in the inn.

Hail Mary/Ave

And there were in the same country shepherds watching, and keeping the night watches over their flock. And behold an angel of the Lord stood by them, and the brightness of God shone round about them; and they feared with a great fear.

Hail Mary/Ave

And the angel said to them: Fear not; for, behold, I bring you good tidings of great joy, that shall be to all the people:

Hail Mary/Ave

For, this day, is born to you a Saviour, who is Christ the Lord, in the city of David.

Hail Mary/Ave

Glory to God in the highest; and on earth peace to men of good will.

Hail Mary/Ave

When When Jesus therefore was born in Bethlehem of Juda, in the days of king Herod, behold, there came wise men from the east to Jerusalem. Saying, Where is he that is born king of the Jews? For we have seen his star in the east, and are come to adore him.

Hail Mary/Ave

"...And behold the star which they had seen in the east, went before them, until it came and stood over where the child was. And seeing the star they rejoiced with exceeding great joy."

Hail Mary/Ave

And entering into the house, they found the child with Mary his mother, and falling down they adored him; and opening their treasures, they offered him gifts; gold, frankincense, and myrrh.

Hail Mary/Ave

But Mary kept all these words, pondering them in her heart.

Hail Mary/Ave

Glory be/Gloria Patri

The Fourth Joyful Mystery - The Presentation

Our Father/Pater noster

And after the days of her purification, according to the law of Moses, were accomplished, they carried him to Jerusalem, to present him to the Lord:

Hail Mary/Ave

And behold there was a man in Jerusalem named Simeon, and this man was just and devout, waiting for the consolation of Israel; and the Holy Ghost was in him.

Hail Mary/Ave

And he had received an answer from the Holy Ghost, that he should not see death, before he had seen the Christ of the Lord.

Hail Mary/Ave

And he came by the Spirit into the temple. And when his parents brought in the child Jesus, to do for him according to the custom of the law, He also took him into his arms, and blessed God, and said:

Hail Mary/Ave

Now thou dost dismiss thy servant, O Lord, according to thy word in peace;

Hail Mary/Ave

Because my eyes have seen thy salvation, Which thou hast prepared before the face of all peoples:

Hail Mary/Ave

A light to the revelation of the Gentiles, and the glory of thy people Israel.

Hail Mary/Ave

And Simeon blessed them, and said to Mary his mother: Behold this child is set for the fall, and for the resurrection of many in Israel, and for a sign which shall be contradicted;

Hail Mary/Ave

And thy own soul a sword shall pierce, that, out of many hearts, thoughts may be revealed.

Hail Mary/Ave

And after they had performed all things according to the law of the Lord, they returned into Galilee, to their city Nazareth. And the child grew, and waxed strong, full of wisdom; and the grace of God was in him.

Hail Mary/Ave

Glory be/Gloria Patri

The Fifth Joyful Mystery - The Finding of Jesus in the Temple

Our Father/Pater noster

And his parents went every year to Jerusalem, at the solemn day of the pasch, And when he was twelve years old, they going up into Jerusalem, according to the custom of the feast,

Hail Mary/Ave

And having fulfilled the days, when they returned, the child Jesus remained in Jerusalem; and his parents knew it not.

Hail Mary/Ave

And not finding him, they returned into Jerusalem, seeking him. And it came to pass, that, after three days, they found him in the temple, sitting in the midst of the doctors, hearing them, and asking them questions.

Hail Mary/Ave

And it came to pass, that, after three days, they found him in the temple, sitting in the midst of the doctors, hearing them, and asking them questions.

Hail Mary/Ave

And all that heard him were astonished at his wisdom and his answers.

Hail Mary/Ave

And seeing him, they wondered. And his mother said to him: Son, why hast thou done so to us? behold thy father and I have sought thee sorrowing.

Hail Mary/Ave

And he said to them: How is it that you sought me? did you not know, that I must be about my father's business?

Hail Mary/Ave

And they understood not the word that he spoke unto them.

Hail Mary/Ave

And he went down with them, and came to Nazareth, and was subject to them. And his mother kept all these words in her heart.

Hail Mary/Ave

And Jesus advanced in wisdom, and age, and grace with God and men.

Hail Mary/Ave

Glory be/Gloria Patri

The Five Sorrowful Mysteries

The First Sorrowful Mystery - The Agony in the Garden

Our Father/Pater noster

Then Jesus came with them into a country place which is called Gethsemani; and he said to his disciples: Sit you here, till I go yonder and pray. And taking with him Peter and the two sons of Zebedee, he began to grow sorrowful and to be sad.

Hail Mary/Ave

Then he saith to them: My soul is sorrowful even unto death:
stay you here, and watch with me.

Hail Mary/Ave

And he was withdrawn away from them a stone's cast; and kneeling down, he prayed,

Hail Mary/Ave

Saying: Father, if thou wilt, remove this chalice from me: but yet not my will, but thine be done.

Hail Mary/Ave

And there appeared to him an angel from heaven, strengthening him. And being in an agony, he prayed the longer.

Hail Mary/Ave

And his sweat became as drops of blood, trickling down upon the ground.

Hail Mary/Ave

And when he rose up from prayer, and was come to his disciples, he found them sleeping for sorrow.

Hail Mary/Ave

And he cometh to his disciples, and findeth them asleep, and he saith to Peter: What? Could you not watch one hour with me?

Hail Mary/Ave

Watch ye, and pray that ye enter not into temptation. The spirit indeed is willing, but the flesh weak.

Hail Mary/Ave

Again the second time, he went and prayed, saying: My Father, if this chalice may not pass away, but I must drink it, thy will be done.

Hail Mary/Ave

Glory be/Gloria Patri

The Second Sorrowful Mystery - The Scourging at the Pillar

Our Father/Pater noster

And straightway in the morning, the chief priests holding a consultation with the ancients and the scribes and the whole council, binding Jesus, led him away, and delivered him to Pilate. And Pilate asked him: Art thou the king of the Jews? But he answering, saith to him: Thou sayest it.

Hail Mary/Ave

Jesus answered: My kingdom is not of this world. If my kingdom were of this world, my servants would certainly strive that I should not be delivered to the Jews: but now my kingdom is not from hence.

Hail Mary/Ave

Pilate therefore said to him: Art thou a king then? Jesus answered: Thou sayest that I am a king. For this was I born, and for this came I into the world; that I should give testimony to the truth. Every one that is of the truth, heareth my voice

Hail Mary/Ave

Pilate saith to him: What is truth? And when he said this, he went out again to the Jews, and saith to them: I find no cause in him.

Hail Mary/Ave

I will chastise him therefore, and release him.
Then therefore, Pilate took Jesus, and scourged him.

Hail Mary/Ave

Despised, and the most abject of men, a man of
sorrows, and acquainted with infirmity: and his look
was as it were hidden and despised, whereupon we
esteemed him not.

Hail Mary/Ave

He was offered because it was his own will,
and he opened not his mouth: he shall be led as a
sheep to the slaughter, and shall be dumb as a lamb
before his shearer, and he shall not open his mouth.

Hail Mary/Ave

But he was wounded for our iniquities, he was
bruised for our sins: the chastisement of our peace
was upon him, and by his bruises we are healed.

Hail Mary/Ave

Surely he hath borne our infirmities and carried our
sorrows: and we have thought him as it were a leper,
and as one struck by God and afflicted.

Hail Mary/Ave

Because his soul hath laboured, he shall see and be
filled: by his knowledge shall this my just servant
justify many, and he shall bear their iniquities.

Hail Mary/Ave

Glory be/Gloria Patri

The Third Sorrowful Mystery - The Crowning with Thorns

Our Father/Pater noster

And the soldiers led him away into the court of the palace, and they called together the whole band: And they clothed him with purple, and platting a crown of thorns, they put it upon him.

Hail Mary/Ave

And stripping him, they put a scarlet cloak about him.

Hail Mary/Ave

And platting a crown of thorns, they put it upon his head, and a reed in his right hand. And bowing the knee before him, they mocked him, saying: Hail, king of the Jews.

Hail Mary/Ave

And spitting upon him, they took the reed, and struck his head.

Hail Mary/Ave

And Pilate seeing that he prevailed nothing, but that rather a tumult was made; taking water washed his hands before the people, saying: I am innocent of the blood of this just man; look you to it.

Hail Mary/Ave

Pilate therefore went forth again, and saith to them: Behold, I bring him forth unto you, that you may know that I find no cause in him. (Jesus therefore came forth, bearing the crown of thorns and the purple garment.) And he saith to them: Behold the Man.

Hail Mary/Ave

But they cried out: Away with him; away with him; crucify him. Pilate saith to them: Shall I crucify your king? The chief priests answered: We have no king but Caesar.

Hail Mary/Ave

And Pilate saith to them: Why, what evil hath he done? But they cried out the more: Crucify him.

Hail Mary/Ave

But they cried out: Away with him; away with him; crucify him.

Hail Mary/Ave

And so Pilate being willing to satisfy the people, released to them Barabbas, and delivered up Jesus, when he had scourged him, to be crucified.

Hail Mary/Ave

Glory be/Gloria Patri

The Fourth Sorrowful Mystery - The Carrying of the Cross

Our Father/Pater noster

And he said to all: If any man will come after me, let him deny himself, and take up his cross daily, and follow me.

Hail Mary/Ave

Then therefore he delivered him to them to be crucified. And they took Jesus, and led him forth.

Hail Mary/Ave

And they forced one Simon a Cyrenian who passed by, coming out of the country, the father of Alexander and of Rufus, to take up his cross.

Hail Mary/Ave

And there followed him a great multitude of people, and of women, who bewailed and lamented him.

Hail Mary/Ave

Take up my yoke upon you, and learn of me,

Hail Mary/Ave

Because I am meek, and humble of heart: and you shall find rest to your souls.

Hail Mary/Ave

For my yoke is sweet and my burden light.

Hail Mary/Ave

But Jesus turning to them, said: Daughters of Jerusalem, weep not over me;

Hail Mary/Ave

But weep for yourselves, and for your children.

Hail Mary/Ave

For if in the green wood they do these things, what shall be done in the dry?

Hail Mary/Ave

Glory be/Gloria Patri

The Fifth Sorrowful Mystery - The Crucifixion

Our Father/Pater noster

And when they were come to the place which is called Calvary, they crucified him there; and the robbers, one on the right hand, and the other on the left.

Hail Mary/Ave

And Jesus said: Father, forgive them, for they know not what they do. But they, dividing his garments, cast lots.

Hail Mary/Ave

And one of those robbers who were hanged, blasphemed him, saying: If thou be Christ, save thyself and us.

Hail Mary/Ave

And Jesus said to him: Amen I say to thee, this day thou shalt be with me in paradise.

Hail Mary/Ave

Now there stood by the cross of Jesus, his mother, and his mother's sister, Mary of Cleophas, and Mary Magdalen. When Jesus therefore had seen his mother and the disciple standing whom he loved, he saith to his mother: Woman, behold thy son.

Hail Mary/Ave

After that, he saith to the disciple: Behold thy mother. And from that hour, the disciple took her to his own.

Hail Mary/Ave

And it was almost the sixth hour; and there was darkness over all the earth until the ninth hour.

Hail Mary/Ave

And Jesus crying out with a loud voice, said: Father, into thy hands I commend my spirit. And saying this, he gave up the ghost.

Hail Mary/Ave

And behold the veil of the temple was rent in two from the top even to the bottom, and the earth quaked, and the rocks were rent.

Hail Mary/Ave

Jesus therefore, when he had taken the vinegar, said: It is consummated. And bowing his head, he gave up the ghost.

Hail Mary/Ave

Glory be/Gloria Patri

The Five Glorious Mysteries

The First Glorious Mystery - The Resurrection

Our Father/Pater noster

Amen, amen I say to you, that you shall lament and weep, but the world shall rejoice; and you shall be made sorrowful, but your sorrow shall be turned into joy.

Hail Mary/Ave

So also you now indeed have sorrow; but I will see you again, and your heart shall rejoice; and your joy no man shall take from you.

Hail Mary/Ave

And on the first day of the week, very early in the morning, they came to the sepulchre, bringing the spices which they had prepared.

Hail Mary/Ave

And behold there was a great earthquake. For an angel of the Lord descended from heaven, and coming, rolled back the stone, and sat upon it.

Hail Mary/Ave

And the angel answering, said to the women: Fear not you; for I know that you seek Jesus who was crucified. He is not here, for he is risen, as he said. Come, and see the place where the Lord was laid.

Hail Mary

He is not here, for he is risen, as he said. Come, and see the place where the Lord was laid. And going quickly, tell ye his disciples that he is risen: and behold he will go before you into Galilee; there you shall see him. Lo, I have foretold it to you.

Hail Mary/Ave

But they going out, fled from the sepulchre. For a trembling and fear had seized them: and they said nothing to any man; for they were afraid. And they went out quickly from the sepulchre with fear and great joy, running to tell his disciples.

Hail Mary/Ave

And they went out quickly from the sepulchre with fear and great joy, running to tell his disciples.

Hail Mary/Ave

I am the resurrection and the life: he that believeth in me, although he be dead, shall live:

Hail Mary/Ave

And every one that liveth, and believeth in me, shall not die for ever. Believest thou this?

Hail Mary/Ave

Glory be/Gloria Patri

The Second Glorious Mystery - The Ascension

Our Father/Pater noster

And he said to them: These are the words which I spoke to you, while I was yet with you, that all things must needs be fulfilled, which are written in the law of Moses, and in the prophets, and in the psalms, concerning me. Then he opened their understanding, that they might understand the scriptures. And he said to them: Thus it is written, and thus it behoved Christ to suffer, and to rise again from the dead, the third day

Hail Mary/Ave

And Jesus coming, spoke to them, saying: All power is given to me in heaven and in earth.

Hail Mary/Ave

Going therefore, teach ye all nations

Hail Mary/Ave

Baptizing them in the name of the Father, and of the Son, and of the Holy Ghost.

Hail Mary/Ave

Teaching them to observe all things whatsoever I have commanded you: and behold I am with you all days, even to the consummation of the world.

Hail Mary/Ave

He that believeth and is baptized, shall be saved: but he that believeth not shall be condemned.

Hail Mary/Ave

And the Lord Jesus, after he had spoken to them, was taken up into heaven, and sitteth on the right hand of God.

Hail Mary/Ave

Behold I am with you all days, even to the consummation of the world.

Hail Mary/Ave

And the Lord Jesus, after he had spoken to them, was taken up into heaven, and sitteth on the right hand of God.

Hail Mary/Ave

But they going forth preached everywhere: the Lord working withal, and confirming the word with signs that followed.

Hail Mary/Ave

The Third Glorious Mystery - The Descent of the Holy Spirit

Our Father/Pater noster

But the Paraclete, the Holy Ghost, whom the Father will send in my name, he will teach you all things, and bring all things to your mind, whatsoever I shall have said to you.

Hail Mary/Ave

And when the days of the Pentecost were accomplished, they were all together in one place

Hail Mary/Ave

And suddenly there came a sound from heaven, as of a mighty wind coming, and it filled the whole house where they were sitting.

Hail Mary/Ave

And there appeared to them parted tongues as it were of fire, and it sat upon every one of them

Hail Mary/Ave

And they were all filled with the Holy Ghost, and they began to speak with divers tongues, according as the Holy Ghost gave them to speak.

Hail Mary/Ave

Now there were dwelling at Jerusalem, Jews, devout men, out of every nation under heaven.

Hail Mary/Ave

And when this was noised abroad, the multitude came together, and were confounded in mind, because that every man heard them speak in his own tongue.

Hail Mary/Ave

But Peter standing up with the eleven, lifted up his voice, and spoke to them: Ye men of Judea, and all you that dwell in Jerusalem, be this known to you, and with your ears receive my words.

Hail Mary/Ave

Peter said to them: Do penance, and be baptized every one of you in the name of Jesus Christ, for the remission of your sins: and you shall receive the gift of the Holy Ghost.

Hail Mary/Ave

They therefore that received his word, were baptized; and there were added in that day about three thousand souls.

Hail Mary/Ave

Glory be/Gloria Patri

The Fourth Glorious Mystery - The Assumption

Our Father/Pater noster

Behold my beloved speaketh to me: Arise, make haste, my love, my dove, my beautiful one, and come.

Hail Mary/Ave

For winter is now past, the rain is over and gone

Hail Mary/Ave

..Shew me thy face, let thy voice sound in my ears: for thy voice is sweet, and thy face comely.

Hail Mary/Ave

And the temple of God was opened in heaven: and the ark of his testament was seen in his temple, and there were lightnings, and voices, and an earthquake, and great hail.

Hail Mary/Ave

And a great sign appeared in heaven: A woman clothed with the sun

Hail Mary/Ave

And the moon under her feet, and on her head a crown of twelve stars

Hail Mary/Ave

Hearken, O daughter, and see, and incline thy ear: and forget thy people and thy father's house. And the king shall greatly desire thy beauty; for he is the Lord thy God, and him they shall adore. All the rich among the people, shall entreat thy countenance. All the glory of the king's daughter is within in golden borders

Hail Mary/Ave

Blessed art thou, O daughter, by the Lord the most high God, above all women upon the earth.

Hail Mary/Ave

Because he hath so magnified thy name this day, that thy praise shall not depart out of the mouth of men who shall be mindful of the power of the Lord for ever,

Hail Mary/Ave

Thou art the glory of Jerusalem, thou art the joy of Israel, thou art the honour of our people

Hail Mary/Ave

Glory be/Gloria Patri

The Fifth Glorious Mystery - The Coronation

Our Father/Pater noster

Who is she that cometh forth as the morning rising, fair as the moon, bright as the sun, terrible as an army set in array?

Hail Mary/Ave

As the rainbow giving light in the bright clouds, and as the flower of roses in the days of the spring, and as the lilies that are on the brink of the water, and as the sweet smelling frankincense in the time of summer.

Hail Mary/Ave

I am the flower of the field, and the lily of the valleys.

Hail Mary/Ave

And in the multitude of the elect she shall have praise, and among the blessed she shall be blessed, saying: I came out of the mouth of the most High, the firstborn before all creatures: I made that in the heavens there should rise light that never faileth, and as a cloud I covered all the earth: I dwelt in the highest places, and my throne is in a pillar of a cloud. I alone have compassed the circuit of heaven, and have penetrated into the bottom of the deep, and have walked in the waves of the sea, And have stood in all the earth: and in every people

Hail Mary/Ave

Come over to me, all ye that desire me, and be filled with my fruits.

Hail Mary/Ave

I was exalted like a cedar in Libanus, and as a cypress tree on mount Sion. I was exalted like a palm tree in Cades, and as a rose plant in Jericho: As a fair olive tree in the plains, and as a plane tree by the water in the streets, was I exalted. I gave a sweet smell like cinnamon and aromatical balm: I yielded a sweet odour like the best myrrh

Hail Mary/Ave

Now therefore, ye children, hear me: Blessed are they that keep my ways. Hear instruction and be wise, and refuse it not.

Hail Mary/Ave

Blessed is the man that heareth me, and that watcheth daily at my gates, and waiteth at the posts of my doors.

Hail Mary/Ave

He that shall find me, shall find life, and shall have salvation from the Lord

Hail Mary/Ave

And a great sign appeared in heaven: A woman clothed with the sun, and the moon under her feet, and on her head a crown of twelve stars

Hail Mary/Ave

Glory be/Gloria Patri

The Litany of the Blessed Virgin

Also called "The Litany of Loreto."

We fly to thy patronage, O holy Mother of God. Despise not our petitions in our necessities: but deliver us from all dangers, O ever glorious and blessed virgin.

Lord, have mercy on us.
Christ have mercy on us.
Lord, have mercy on us.
Christ hear us.
Christ, graciously hear us.
God the Father of heaven, *have mercy on us.*
God the Son, Redeemer of the world, *have mercy on us.*
God the Holy Ghost, *have mercy on us.*
Holy Trinity, one God, *have mercy on us.*

Holy Mary, *Pray for us.*
Holy Mother of God,
Holy Virgin of virgins,
Mother of Christ,
Mother of divine grace,
Mother most pure,
Mother most chaste,
Mother inviolate,
Mother undefiled,
Mother most amiable,
Mother most admirable,
Mother of our Creator,
Mother of our Redeemer,

Virgin most prudent,
Virgin most venerable,
Virgin most renowned,
Virgin most powerful,
Virgin most merciful,
Virgin most faithful,
Mirror of justice,
Seat of wisdom,
Cause of our joy,
Spiritual Vessel,
Vessel of honor,
Singular vessel of devotion,
Mystical rose,
Tower of David,
Tower of ivory,
House of gold,

Ark of the covenant,
Gate of heaven,
Morning star,
Health of the sick,
Refuge of sinners,
Comforter of the afflicted,
Help of Christians,
Queen of Angels,
Queen of Patriarchs,
Queen of Prophets,
Queen of Apostles,
Queen of Martyrs,
Queen of Confessors,
Queen of Virgins,
Queen of all Saints,
Queen conceived without original sin,
Queen of the most holy Rosary,
Queen of Peace,

Lamb of God, Who takest away the sins of the world, *spare us, O Lord.*

Lamb of God, Who takest away the sins of the world, *graciously hear us, O Lord.*

Lamb of God, Who takest away the sins of the world, *have mercy on us, O Lord.*

P. Pray for us, O holy Mother of God.

S. That we may be made worthy of the promises of Christ.

LET US PRAY

Pour forth, we beseech Thee, O Lord, Thy grace into our hearts; that as we have known the Incarnation of Christ Thy Son, by the message of an angel, so, by His Passion and Cross, we may be brought to the glory of His resurrection: through the same Christ, our Lord. Amen.

A Rosary Office for the Dead

Make the sign of the cross with the Glory Be/Gloria Patri

Say, "Let us pray for the souls of (say names)/"

Say the Our Father/Pater noster

Say Three Hail Marys/Aves

Say "Eternal rest unto them, Oh Lord, and let light perpetual shine upon them. May their souls, with all the souls of the faithful departed, Rest in Peace. Amen."

Recite the Rosary according to the Glorious Mysteries, adding the Eternal Rest prayer at the end of each decade.

Recite the De Profundis (Psalm 130) and end with a Glory Be/Gloria patri.

De Profundis

Out of the depths I have cried to thee, O Lord: Lord, hear my voice. Let thy ears be attentive to the voice of my supplication. If thou, O Lord, wilt mark iniquities: Lord, who shall stand it. For with thee there is merciful forgiveness: and by reason of thy law, I have waited for thee, O Lord. My soul hath relied on his word: My soul hath hoped in the Lord. From the morning watch even until night, let Israel hope in the Lord. Because with the Lord there is mercy: and with him plentiful redemption. And he shall redeem Israel from all his iniquities.

Memorare

Remember, O most gracious Virgin Mary, that never was it known that anyone who fled to they protection, implored they help, or sought thy intercession was left unaided. Inspired with this confidence, I fly unto thee, O Virgin of virgins, my Mother. To thee I come, before thee I stand, sinful and sorrowful. O Mother of the Word Incarnate, despise not my petitions, but in thy mercy hear and answer me. Amen.

The Angelus

V. The angel of the Lord declared unto Mary.
R. And she conceived by the Holy Ghost.

Hail Mary/Ave

V. Behold the handmaid of the Lord.
R. Be it done to me according to thy word.

Hail Mary/Ave

V. And the Word was made flesh.
R. And dwelt among us.

Hail Mary/Ave

V. Pray for us, O Holy Mother of God.
R. That we may be made worthy of the promises of Christ.

Let us pray. Pour forth, we beseech thee, O Lord, Thy grace into our hearts, that we to whom the Incarnation of Christ, Thy Son, was made known by the message of an angel, may by His passion and cross be brought to the glory of his resurrection, through the same Christ Our Lord. Amen

May the divine assistance remain always with us.

And may the souls of the faithful departed through the mercy of God rest in peace. Amen.

Regina Caeli

Queen of heaven, rejoice, alleluia.
The Son you merited to bear, alleluia,
Has risen as he said, alleluia.
Pray to God for us, alleluia.

Regina Caeli in Latin

Regina caeli, laetare, alleluia;
Quia quem meruisti portare, alleluia,
Resurrexit, sicut dixit, alleluia:
Ora pro nobis Deum, alleluia.

The Magnificat

My soul doth magnify the Lord,
And my spirit hath rejoiced in God my Saviour
Because He hath regarded the humility of his
handmaid: for behold from henceforth all generations
shall call me blessed.
Because He that is mighty hath done great things to
me, and holy is His name.
And His mercy is from generation unto generations to
them that fear Him.
He hath shewed might in His arm: He hath scattered
the proud in the conceit of their heart.
He hath put down the mighty from their seat, and hath
exalted the humble.
He hath filled the hungry with good things, and the
rich he hath sent empty away.
He hath received Israel His servant, being mindful of
His mercy.
As He spoke to our fathers; to Abraham and his seed
forever.

Glory be to the Father, and to the Son, and to the
Holy Ghost, as it was in the beginning is now, and
ever shall be, world without end. Amen.

The Magnificat in Latin

Magnificat anima mea Dominum;
Et exsultavit spiritus meus in Deo salutari meo,
Quia respexit humilitatem ancillae suae; ecce enim ex
hoc beatam me dicent omnes generationes.
Quia fecit mihi magna qui potens est, et sanctum
nomen ejus,
Et misericordia ejus a progenie in progenies
timentibus eum.
Fecit potentiam in bracchio suo;
Dispersit superbos mente cordis sui.
Deposuit potentes de sede, et exaltavit humiles.
Esurientes implevit bonis, et divites dimisit inanes.
Suscepit Israel, puerum suum, recordatus
misericordiae suae,
Sicut locutus est ad patres nostros, Abraham et semini
ejus in saecula.

Gloria Patri, et Filio, et Spiritui Sancto,: sicut erat in
principio, Et nunc, et semper: et in Saecula
saeculorum. Amen.

Printed in Great Britain
by Amazon